SPLASH 2
DISCIPLESHIP

SPLASH
DISCIPLESHIP 2

Ken Hemphill

Auxano
PRESS
Tigerville, South Carolina
www.AuxanoPress.com

ISBN 978-0-578-04445-3

Published by Auxano Press
Tigerville, South Carolina
www.AuxanoPress.com

To order additional copies, contact Ken Hemphill, Auxano Press, P.O. Box 315,
Tigerville, SC 29688; or order online to www.auxanopress.com.

For additional resources for this and other studies, go to
www.auxanopress.com or contact Ken Hemphill,
Auxano Press, P.O. Box 315, Tigerville, SC 29688.

*I dedicate this book to
my students at
Southern Baptist Theological Seminary
and
North Greenville University
who have*

*challenged me to
think outside the box
as we have explored a
new strategy for discipling.*

CONTENTS

ABOUT THE AUTHOR

Ken serves as the National Strategist for
Empowering Kingdom Growth, Southern
Baptist Convention. His passion is to advance
the Kingdom of God by honoring kingdom
principles set forth in God's Word. His heart
is for the local church, and to see pastors and
ministers succeed in their ministry role.

PREFACE

YOU CAN BE A GROWTH COACH

Congratulations, you have this book in your hand because you want to grow in your relationship with Christ and, in turn, help others to grow. You may be planning to use it as a family project for personal enrichment and the spiritual maturation of your children. You may be reading through it because God has used you to lead a family member, friend, or colleague to faith in Jesus Christ. *This little book is designed to be your guidebook as you walk together with a friend. You will discover that both of you will develop a more intimate walk with Christ.* You should use this book as a manual to help another. Don't just give it to the new believer and hope they will make their way through it on their own. You must become their growth coach.

Why?

It would be artificial and disingenuous to *splash* someone to faith in Christ and then not assist them in their spiritual growth. What if someone established an ongoing relationship with you and became the instrument God used to bring you to a faith commitment to Christ, then simply abandoned you after they introduced you to Christ? You would feel unsupported, perhaps discarded. You might even begin to doubt the authenticity and importance of the commitment you made. I know you don't want any doubts to arise in the mind or heart of the person you have led to a faith commitment.

It is your *privilege* and *responsibility* to nurture the faith of someone you lead to Christ. We are rightly appalled when we hear about someone who gives birth to a child and then abandons that child. I read recently of a young mother who placed a living child in a dumpster behind her apartment building. What a travesty! "Human life is sacred," we cry. It's true and nothing could be more sacred than the new spiritual life that has been birthed in the person who prays to receive Christ as their Savior.

The friend who you led to Christ is like a newborn babe and they cannot be abandoned. They will soon encounter the struggle between their old nature and their new nature. They need your help to know how to win this battle. They will experience the spiritual hunger for God's Word and they need your help to feed them and then to teach them how to feed themselves from the pure milk of God's Word. Here's how Peter referred to the hunger of the new believer. "Like newborn babies. Long for the pure milk of the word, so that by it you may grow in respect to salvation" (1 Peter 2:2).

Here's some really good news that will encourage you. The excitement that accompanies the new birth will provide the natural platform for the discussion of issues of spiritual growth. In other words, your friend will be eager for you to help him in the process of growth. Genuine conversion creates a supernatural hunger for spiritual food.

What?

In the *SPLASH* ministry process, you have spoken informally and casually about your personal relationship to Christ. God used this conversational and relational approach to bring about the new birth commitment and you can trust Him to use the same process to continue the discipling process. This will be a casual, informal, and natural approach to spiritual maturation. The entire process should be joyous for both of you.

In *SPLASH* you learned to *demonstrate* and *articulate* the Gospel. The discipling process involves both concepts once again. When you initiate the process of discipling, you are actually demonstrating what it means to be a fully committed follower of Christ. You will show your friend how to read Scripture as well as tell him principles of interpreting and understanding Scripture. The same will be true of prayer and other spiritual disciplines.

We recommend that you **not** announce—"Now that you are a Christian, I am going to disciple you." Such a statement would probably frighten your friend and might intimidate you. Don't give the impression that you are the spiritual giant who is helping a struggling new believer. You are a friend who desires to walk the Christian journey together with a new member of your spiritual family. We suggest you make no "announcement" at all.

You will simply and naturally continue the conversation about how one can have a growing personal relationship with Christ. Your first conversation after the prayer of commitment may be as simple as asking, "Tell me what has happened since you prayed to receive Christ?" Or you might ask, "Do you have any questions about the commitment you made last week?"

We are going to give you several steps based on the acrostic *SPLASH*. In this instance it stands for **Scripture, Prayer, Love, Accountability, Stewardship, and Heart.** We have used the same acrostic because we like to keep things simple. Don't look at these as sequential steps that you must take one after the other. They may run together as you talk about growing in relationship with Christ. In certain instances you may begin mid-way in the sequence based on the need, background, and interest of the individual involved. In other words, one person may have an immediate interest in prayer; another may need an accountability partner. Feel free to customize the *SPLASH* discipling process to meet the need of the moment.

Much of the flow of the process will be determined by the unique needs of the person involved. You will ask questions, which we will provide, and your friend's answers will guide you to the next step. Another clue concerning how to proceed will be questions your friend may ask you as he begins to grow. Relax. We will provide help with appropriate answers.

When and Where?

You may be thinking, "I am too busy to take on a task like this—when and how often do I need to meet." First, you should not look at this as a chore you must do but as a privilege you are allowed to do. Second, you have been walking with this friend through the spiritual birth process and thus you should see this as an extension of that process. Since it is *informal* we suggest you follow a plan that seems most convenient to the two of you.

If you developed your relationship at the fitness center or at your children's soccer practice, continue the discipling process there if that is most appropriate. If you are separated by distance, you can use the phone or e-mail to assist you in the process. Don't let the when and where become issues that present barriers that might keep you from embarking on the joyous journey of discipling another person.

Relax and Enjoy!

You may be thinking, "I'm not competent to disciple another person." If God can use you to lead someone to develop a relationship with His Son, He can use you to deepen that relationship. Discipling another person does not assume that you have "arrived" in your own spiritual walk. If it did, we would all be disqualified. In truth, you will find that your faith relationship will grow as a result of your participation in the discipling process.

Discipleship is a journey of faith and transformation. Do not become discouraged. Remember, your growth to this point has been a process with "ups," "downs," "pauses," and "interruptions." Be patient and transparent. Don't be afraid to share your own story, with all its imperfections. Remember sharing your story is what God used to bring this person to Christ and He will use "the rest of your story" in the discipling process.

You are not alone in this process. Your church family will come alongside to assist you. In the process, we encourage you to take your new friend to a small group Bible study and worship celebration to help them grow in their faith and develop a broader context of accountability. Don't forget that Scripture has power to transform and we will be using Scripture throughout the process. Be assured that the Holy Spirit will guide and inform you. In the original *SPLASH* study you learned to rely upon and sense the direction of the Holy Spirit, you can trust Him to be your encourager and guide now.

Seven Reminders
1. Be assured the Holy Spirit will empower and guide you.
2. Trust the power of Scripture to accomplish the work of discipleship.
3. Use the model suggested, but do not become a slave to it. Customize!
4. Be informal and conversational.
5. Seek natural opportunities to help your friend find a community of faith.
6. As you meet with your friend you will be demonstrating what it means to be a disciple.

7. Use simple open-ended questions to help
    determine spiritual needs.

How?

In our *SPLASH* ministry process we followed the
model of Jesus and we will do the same when it comes
to developing disciples. Our model comes from an
overview of the life of Jesus, but can be found in a
succinct form in Matthew 9:35-10:42. You will benefit
from taking a few moments to read the entire passage.
To simply the process we will look at it using five words
that begin with "E."

*   **Embody.** What Jesus teaches in Matthew 10 is
    what He has been doing with the disciples. He
    sends them out to declare the good news of the
    kingdom, the very thing He has been doing in
    their presence. People learn more by observing you
    than they do from listening to you. This process
    requires that you spend time with the person you
    are coaching.

*   **Evaluate.** Jesus knew His disciples well. He knew
    that they would be tested and they would fail in some
    of their tests. You have already begun a relationship
    that will help you evaluate the spiritual needs
    of the person you are joining in the discipleship
    journey. You can ask key questions to assist you
    in the evaluation process. "What is your religious
    background?" "Have you ever attended church?"
    "What did you think of those experiences?" "Have
    you ever read the Bible?" "What questions did it
    raise?" "Have you ever prayed?" "What happened?"
    You will think of other questions as the Holy

Spirit prompts you. Evaluation will allow you to customize the discipling process.

- **Equip.** Jesus constantly instructed His disciples in what to do and how to accomplish it. The *SPLASH* outline and discussion that follows will provide you with valuable tools that will enable you to equip others to walk in intimate fellowship with Christ.

- **Examine.** The Lord watched and examined the work of His disciples to allow Him to refine them in their walk. You do this through observation and friendly interrogation. You will need to ask about progress challenges. Be open to hear and ready to gently correct, redirect, and encourage. Watch to see transformation take place and be ready to point out the progress you are seeing.

- **Encourage.** Examination, evaluation, and correction should never be viewed in a negative light either by you or the friend you have joined in the discipleship journey. You are to be an encourager. Pick your friend up when he has fallen, pat him on the back, and push him ahead when he succeeds. William Arthur Ward said, "Flatter me, and I may not believe you. Criticize me, and I may not like you. Ignore me, and I may not forgive you. Encourage me, and I will not forget you."

A helpful tool that you may enjoy reading as an encouragement to you is *The Master Plan of Evangelism* by Robert E. Coleman (Revell).

A DISCIPLER'S GUIDE

CHAPTER 1

SCRIPTURE

We begin with Scripture because it is the essential tool of the discipling process. Remember Scripture was the key tool in our witnessing strategy. It is the primary means through which we hear God speak and learn His ways.

The Bible, the written record of God's revelation of Himself to mankind, is crucial to our understanding of God and the world that He created. The Bible doesn't simply add to our theological knowledge, it is central to all knowledge, for in it we encounter the only true living God who acts on man's behalf. We may learn about God from observing nature and through our own conscience, but the Bible is the only complete source for knowing about God and His plan for our life. It is consistent for us to speak about Christ as the living Word of God (John 1:1) and the Bible as the written Word of God.

Throughout the history of the church, leaders have spoken of Scripture as the only final and sufficient rule of faith and practice. For this reason Scripture

1

becomes the final authority and the point of reference by which all beliefs and their accompanying behavior patterns must be evaluated. Belief should always impact behavior. Thus we study Scripture not simply for information but for transformation.

In this chapter we will look at a few simple truths about Scripture that you should cover with your friend. After a discussion of this background material, I will give you questions to ask and suggestions to make to your friend.

Essential Truths about Scripture

The Bible is God's revelation to man. When we think of Scripture, we should first ask how an infinite God would speak to finite humans. In Romans 1:19-20, Paul indicates that God reveals Himself in nature and through the human conscience. But man requires a more direct revelation to more completely understand the will of God. The Bible is God's spoken word to man. Both the Old and New Testaments tell the story of God's redemptive activity in history.

The writer of Hebrews states that God spoke first through His prophets and finally and fully in His Son. "God, after He spoke long ago to the fathers in the prophets in many portions and in many ways, in these last days has spoken to us in His Son, whom He appointed heir of all things, through whom also He made the world. And He is the radiance of His glory and the exact representation of His nature, and upholds all things by the word of His power" (1:1-3a). Since Jesus is fully God, nothing can be added to the full revelation we have in our hands when we study the Bible. If your friend asks about any of the "lost" or "forgotten" books that are sometimes the source for popular movies, you can take him to this verse.

Peter tells us that the *content* of Scripture came from God and not from the human instrument that recorded God's revelation. "But know this first of all, that no prophecy of Scripture is a matter of one's own interpretation, for no prophecy was ever made by an act of human will, but men moved by the Holy Spirit spoke from God" (2 Peter 1:20-21). David clearly indicated that what he spoke was words given by God. "The Spirit of the Lord spoke through me, his word was on my tongue" (2 Samuel 23:2)(NIV). The prophet Jeremiah made this same point graphically—"Then the Lord reached out his hand and touched my mouth and said to me, 'Now, I have put my words in your mouth'" (1:9) (NIV).

The knowledge, that the Bible allows us to hear the very words of God, gives us great confidence that we can know and live by God's standards. The Bible will enable us to assist others in their spiritual growth. Good news—you are not dependent upon your strength and wisdom in the discipling process. Let God's Word do its work.

Use the verses above to explain to a new believer that the Bible is no ordinary book. It contains the very words of God and speaks to every area of one's life. I would suggest that you read these verses together and underline them in your Bible and that of your friend. Choose several texts from this chapter for Scripture memory.

The Bible is inspired. The word "inspiration" refers to the *transmission* of the content of Scripture from God to humanity through those who spoke and recorded these messages. Second Timothy 3:16 teaches us, "All Scripture is inspired by God...." Some translations read "God-breathed" indicating that both the source of Scripture and the means of transmission were accomplished by God.

This same truth is underlined in 2 Peter 1:21. "Prophecy never had its origin in the will of man, but men spoke from God as they were carried along by the Holy Spirit" (NIV). The phrase "spoke from God" refers to *revelation*, indicating the content originates with God and "carried along by the Holy Spirit" points to *inspiration*. In other words, God prompted men to speak and write, gave them the words, and carried them along in the process of speaking and recording His words.

The Bible, distinct from other "holy books," was not an act of human initiative. It does not record man's attempt to find or explain God, but God's revelation of Himself to man. God did not destroy the personality of the human instrument, but rather guided, controlled, and protected them from error. Since God chose to use human authors, they spoke and wrote in the normal language and idioms of their day. They used figures of speech and illustrations common to their times and geographical locations. As you read the prophetic books, gospels, or letters of Paul you will find that styles of writing vary greatly. God was willing to speak to man in a manner that he could fully and easily understand.

You can use the truth of "inspiration" to explain

how the Bible was given to man and kept free from error. This truth not only gives us confidence in God's Word, it assures us that God will inform our minds as we read and study His Word today.

The Bible is trustworthy. It is important that you help the friend you are guiding through the discipling process to understand that the Bible is both accurate and trustworthy. This is more critical today than ever before because of the truth claims made about other books such as the Koran or the Book of Mormon. Further, many persons in modern day society are reluctant to believe that any one book can claim to present absolute truth.

When we speak of the Bible as both accurate and trustworthy, we can use the words *inerrant* and *infallible*. Common usage makes little distinction between the two terms. In classical usage *infallibility* signifies the full trustworthiness of a guide that is not deceived and does not deceive. Think of it in these terms—if you were going on a journey into a wilderness area unknown to you, you would hire a guide. You would probably check references to find out whether this guide was trustworthy or deceptive or easily deceived. If your very survival depended on this guide, his trustworthiness is no small matter.

Explain to your friend that the quality of our earthly life and our eternal destiny depends upon the trustworthiness of our guide, the Bible. We can rejoice because we know it is trustworthy. Nothing in the Bible will ever mislead us and thus we can obey it with joyous abandon.

Inerrancy speaks of the *truthfulness* of a source of information. In other words, does the information contain mistakes? When we speak of the Bible as inerrant, we are affirming that—when properly understood in the context of its ancient cultural form and content, it is completely truthful in all it says about God's will and way. If the Bible contains errors, then man would need someone sufficiently brilliant to detect which passages are flawed and which are reliable. God so loved the world, that He did not leave man with a book that required him to pick out the reliable parts from the unreliable.

Let's again think about our trip into the unknown wilderness with our guide. We have established that the guide is trustworthy. But what if the map our guide used was flawed? Even though he intended to guide us safely, he would lead us astray. The knowledge that our map—our Bible—is completely *truthful* gives us confidence in life and death.

As you assist someone in the discipling process, you can help them gain assurance of the reliability of the Bible by asking and answering two questions. First, "If God desired to reveal Himself to man, *would* He do so in a totally accurate (inerrant) and reliable (infallible) way?" The word *would* indicates the "intent" or "desire" of God. The only possible answer is "yes" for the God revealed in Scripture is neither deceitful nor capricious. He is not a "trickster" like the Roman gods. The God of the Bible is truthful and perfect and thus *would* make Himself known in a manner consistent with His own nature. If such is not true, man is in a hopeless situation, for he is unqualified to match wits with a god who has no desire to reveal himself in an accurate and reliable way.

Once we have resolved the first question, we must move to a related question. "*Could* God protect and preserve His revelation of Himself to man?" The word *could* speaks to "ability." Some liberal scholars argue that we cannot claim to have an inerrant text because God used fallible human instruments to record His revelation of Himself. However, such an argument leaves us in an impossible situation. We have a God who *desires* to reveal Himself to His own creation in a reliable and accurate manner, but is *incapable* of doing so. In other words, God is *finite* or limited in His ability. Yet, a limited god is not the God of the Bible.

Could not the God who created the world, entered that world in human flesh through His Son, and raised Christ from the grave also protect His written revelation from error? To suggest that He could not do so is both a weak and illogical position since the writers of Scripture would then have created (in their own minds) a God who is mightier than the One that they affirm prompted them to write. When we conclude that God both *would* and *could* protect His Word, we are left with the historical position of evangelical Christianity—the Bible is the inerrant and infallible record of God's revelation to man.

Thus, in our discipling process, we start from a position of strength as we speak about issues of life and eternity. We have a trustworthy word from the Creator and Author of life. When inerrancy is rejected, we are less sure of the value of Scripture, less certain of our own faith, and more susceptible to alternative truth claims. Thus, we must begin with simple affirmation of the authority, truthfulness, and sufficiency of God's Word.

The Bible is powerful. While the issues of revelation, inspiration, and trustworthiness are important to all believers, the truth that the Bible is *powerful* will provide both the motivation to study the Bible and the confidence to obey it. We can read a great classic and be moved to tears and inspired, but no other book has the power to transform us. No single book has impacted mankind throughout the centuries as the Bible has.

Here are a few statements, about the power inherent in God's Word, that are worth committing to memory. Purchase some 3x5 cards and print these verses on them and share them with your friend. Work on memorizing these together.

- The Word will accomplish God's purpose. "For as the rain and the snow come down from heaven, and do not return there without watering the earth and making it bear and sprout, and furnishing seed to the sower and bread to the eater; so will My word be which goes forth from My mouth; it will not return to Me empty, without accomplishing what I desire, and without succeeding in the matter for which I sent it" (Isaiah 55:10-11).

- The Word will provide guidance. "Your word is a lamp unto my feet and a light to my path" (Psalm 119:105).

- The Word is the power for salvation. "For I am not ashamed of the gospel, for it is the power of God for salvation to everyone who believes, to the Jew first and also to the Greek" (Romans 1:16).

- The Word teaches, rebukes, corrects, and directs. "All Scripture is inspired by God and profitable for teaching, for reproof, for correction, for training in righteousness; so that the man of God may be adequate, equipped for every good work" (2 Timothy 3:16-17).

- The Word judges our thoughts and attitudes. "For the word of God is living and active and sharper than any two-edged sword, and piercing as far as the division of soul and spirit, of both joints and marrow, and able to judge the thoughts and intentions of the heart" (Hebrews 4:12).

All of these verses indicate that the Word has the power to accomplish the stated result. This should give you comfort as you share the discipleship journey with a friend. You are neither capable nor responsible for changing the life of another person, but God's Word is sufficient.

What about all the contradictions in the Bible? You may be concerned that you will be asked about the "supposed" errors and contradictions in the Bible. Most "objections" about biblical accuracy arise from immaterial or uninformed impressions. Most are the result of exposure to negative attitudes about the Bible rather than firsthand investigation of its contents. Your positive approach to the Word plus the indwelling presence of the Holy Spirit in the life of your friend will be sufficient to deal with most questions and concerns. We have provided a link to helpful websites on splashinfo.com if there are questions you want to explore together. Another good resource is *The Encyclopedia of Bible Difficulties* by Gleason L. Archer.

You may find that it is more productive to focus on the evidence of the uniqueness of the Bible rather than trying to solve difficulties. The original Biblical documents would be called the "autographs." We do not possess any of the original autographs. The same would be true for any other document from the time of the writing of the Bible. We do have a large number of quality early manuscripts. In the case of the Old Testament, the Hebrew texts are unusually well preserved. They have proved themselves to be exceptionally reliable and have been supported by the Dead Sea Scrolls.

With more than 5,000 Greek and 8,000 Latin manuscripts, no other book in ancient literature can compare with the New Testament in documentary support. For example, we have only seven early copies of Plato's writings, five of Aristotle's and 643 of Homer's. It is fascinating that some college professors, who love to cast doubt on the reliability of the Bible by citing issues related to manuscript copies, accept without question the reliability of the manuscripts of Aristotle or Plato.

The quality of the various New Testament manuscripts is without parallel in the ancient world. The reverence the Jewish scribes and early Christian copyists had for Scripture caused them to exercise extreme caution as they copied and preserved the authentic text. Because we do have thousands of manuscripts, readings may vary in places; but the differences are often little more than spellings of names—the result of visual or auditory errors in the copying process. Only a minute number would affect one's understanding of the text and none call into question a major doctrine or factual teaching.

Two other strong arguments for the reliability of the Bible are the findings of archaeology and fulfilled prophecy. Sir William Ramsay, a wealthy atheist with a doctorate from Oxford University, devoted much of his life to archaeological study with the desire to disprove the Bible. After 25 years of work, he became so impressed with the historical accuracy of Luke and Acts, he shocked the world by declaring that he had become a Christian.

The Old Testament contains numerous specific prophecies about events fulfilled during the time of the writing of the Bible. They are so detailed and specific they could not be educated guesses. Often, the prophet predicted the opposite of what one would have anticipated.

The Bible was uniquely produced, involving more than 40 authors over a span of more than 1,500 years. Authors included a king, shepherds, a tax collector, a fisherman, a physician and a Pharisee turned missionary. Their diversity, reflected in their educational levels and socioeconomic lifestyles, is evident in their writings. These authors employ virtually every known literary form. Yet, the Bible has a harmonious, continuous, and complete story that flows from creation to consummation. A modern day publisher would never consider inviting 40 different authors from different eras and different levels of ability to write on a particular theme and then bind their 66 books together as one single book. The Bible bears witness to its divine authorship.

Getting Started

The materials we have just covered concerning the essentials of the Bible were written with you in mind. These are essential truths that we need to have as our foundation as we begin to disciple another. Feel free to talk about these issues as they emerge naturally from your conversation. Each person that you have the privilege to disciple will begin with a different level of understanding and therefore your discipling strategy will be dependent upon their need and interest.

You have already discovered in the *SPLASH* evangelism strategy that the Holy Spirit will guide you as you talk with your friend about spiritual truths. Before you enter into any discipling dialogue, ask the Spirit to give you the words to say. As you begin each session with your friend, pray for guidance. Your open dependence on the Spirit is an important truth that you will demonstrate. "Showing" is as important to discipleship as it was to evangelism.

Ask questions to determine where to start. You may want to begin by sharing a little of your own story about how you learned to study the Bible for yourself. Don't be afraid to speak about your own personal struggles. Your honesty will greatly allay the fears of a new believer that they will never master the Bible. After sharing your story, begin to explore what knowledge your friend has concerning the Bible. Here are a few good questions. Feel free to add others.

- Have you ever attempted to read the Bible for yourself?
- What books of the Bible have you read?
- Did you understand what you read?
- What translation(s) of the Bible do you own?
- Would you like for me to share with you some of the tools that have helped me to study and understand the Bible?

Based on the responses to these questions, and others you might ask, you will have an idea of where to begin your discussion of studying the Bible. Do not ask these questions in a demeaning fashion, but do not assume that any question is too basic to ask. Your attitude must be one of a servant who only desires to assist a fellow traveler in the Christian journey.

Choosing a Bible. You may need to begin by explaining what is meant by a "translation." At the most basic level, anyone who does not read the Hebrew and Greek texts will read from a translation. There are many good translations available to the Bible student today. Essentially three different options are open to the reader—word for word, thought for thought, and paraphrase.

The "word for word" translation is sometimes called a "literal translation" or a "formal equivalence." Examples of the formal equivalence would be The

King James, The New King James, The New American Standard, The Holman Christian Standard, The Revised Standard, and the English Standard Bible. Word for word translations attempt to preserve the original syntax and exact meaning of the words without sacrificing readability. As an individual grows in their Bible study skills, they will probably want to own several translations, and a "formal equivalence" should be included in their collection.

At the other end of the spectrum from the "word for word" translation is the "paraphrase." The original Living Bible by Kenneth Taylor, The Good News for Modern Man, and The Cotton Patch are examples of popular paraphrases. The paraphrase takes great liberty with the text, and thus may be acceptable for devotional reading, but does not make a good study Bible.

The "dynamic equivalence" lies between the "formal equivalence" and the paraphrase. The translators attempt to make the Bible more readable by translating thought for thought without moving into paraphrasing. The New International Version, The New English Bible, J.B. Phillips' New Testament in Modern English, and the New Living Bible are examples of dynamic equivalence.

This information will help your friend choose a Bible. You might want to offer to accompany your friend on a trip to the local Christian bookstore to purchase a Bible if he expresses a desire and need for a new Bible. You may be thinking, "Which of the above options should I recommend?" First, you can tell him which translation you prefer and why. Second, you can ask a bookstore employee to assist. Third, have your friend pick a passage he is familiar with and read it in several translations so he can get a feel for a particular translation. I would suggest that you lead him to choose either a "formal equivalence" or "dynamic equivalence" for his study Bible.

As you shop together for a Bible, you may also want to talk about other tools available in many Bibles. Study Bibles contain introductory articles, chapter outlines, commentary notes, concordances, and maps. The primary advantage of the study Bible is that it puts a host of useful tools in a single location. The possible drawback is that it may be a "bit overwhelming" to a new believer. You should also remember that the notes are the words of man and thus not inerrant.

Help them to become familiar with their Bible. Whatever translation your friend chooses, I would encourage you to help him become familiar with his Bible. Start with the table of contents. Here you can discuss the division of the Bible into two covenants or testaments, the Old and the New. Both contain salvation history and both are fully inspired and reliable. The Old Testament contains 39 books while the New has 27. The Old Testament contains the promise of the Messiah; the New Testament contains the fulfillment of that promise. The table of contents will assist your friend in finding books that may not be that familiar to him.

The first five books of the Old Testament are referred to as the Pentateuch or Torah. These books cover the story of salvation history from the very beginning until the entry into the Promised Land. These five books are foundational and fundamental, including the story of the Patriarchs, the redemption from Egyptian bondage, and the giving of the Law.

The Pentateuch is followed by twelve historical books, beginning with Joshua and ending with Esther. These books continue the story of God's people beginning with the entry into the Promised Land. They recount the time of the Judges and the Kings (including the united and divided kingdoms), the Babylonian captivity, and the return from exile.

In the middle of the Old Testament are the five books of poetry which include Job, Psalms, Proverbs, Ecclesiastes, and Song of Solomon. These books contain wisdom literature.

The final two sections are the Major Prophets, including Isaiah, Jeremiah, Lamentations, Ezekiel, and Daniel. The writings of the Minor Prophets begin with Hosea and conclude with Malachi. The chief difference between major and minor prophets is the length of their books. It has nothing to do with their relative value.

The prophets were spokesmen for God. Much of the content of their message was intended for the people and time in which they lived. However, some of their messages contained prophecy which was yet to come, including the promise of the coming Messiah.

The New Testament begins with the four gospels, plus Acts which provides the historical framework. Matthew, Mark, and Luke are referred to as the synoptic gospels, because they view the life of Christ from a chronological perspective. John organizes his work around significant "sign" events in the life of Jesus. Luke and Acts is actually a two-volume work by a single author, Luke. Luke tells the life of Christ from beginning through the resurrection and Acts tells us of the birth and empowering of the church as the continuation of the ministry of Christ.

The Apostle Paul wrote thirteen of our New Testament letters generally referred to as the Pauline letters. Most were letters addressed to early churches which he planted as the first great missionary. Letters such as those to Timothy, Titus, and Philemon are more personal in nature.

The general epistles include Hebrews, James, First and Second Peter, First, Second, and Third John, and Jude. The final book is Revelation, which tells of the culmination of all things.

It may be helpful to suggest that your friend mark these divisions on the table of contents in his Bible to assist him in remembering the basic divisions of the Bible.

The Big Picture

Before you discuss the basic tools of Bible study, it might be helpful to provide a big picture of the Bible from beginning to end. There are several ways we could proceed with this overview of the Bible, but I am going to follow a pattern given by Vaughn Roberts in his book *God's Big Picture*, a great book to own.

Vaughn bases his overview on the theme of the kingdom of God, the dominant theme of Jesus' teaching ministry. Jesus cast His mission in terms of fulfilling the promises of the kingdom as fulfillment of the prophecies of the Old Testament. Although the term "kingdom of God" does not appear in the Old Testament, the idea certainly does. Vaughn indicates that he is following Graeme Goldsworthy, who presents the kingdom as the over-arching theme of the whole Bible. I will provide a simple synthesis of Vaughn's conclusions to help you understand the big picture of God's work to establish His rule and reign among His people.

Here is a brief synopsis of the big picture of God's kingdom activity from beginning to end.

The Old Testament

The pattern of the kingdom. The Garden of Eden establishes the pattern of the kingdom. Adam and Eve are allowed to live in God's place under His rule at they submit to His word. To be under God's rule is to enjoy His blessing. This is God's design for man and thus the best way to live.

The perished kingdom. Tragically, Adam and Eve believe they can live more abundantly by ignoring God's rule. The results are tragic as they turn away from God. They forfeit God's place as they are banished from the garden. They forfeit God's blessings when they remove themselves from God's rule. While the situation seems desperate, God is determined to restore His kingdom.

The promised kingdom. God makes a covenant with Abraham and his descendants that includes His plan to re-establish His kingdom. They are to live in

His land and enjoy His blessing so that all the people of the earth will be blessed through them.

The partial kingdom. The Bible shows how God's promises to Abraham are partially fulfilled in the history of Israel. By redeeming Israel from Egyptian bondage, God makes Abraham's descendants His own people. At Mount Sinai, He gives them His law so they can live under His rule and enjoy His blessing. This blessing is marked by God's presence with and among His people as symbolized in the tabernacle. Under Joshua's leadership, they enter the Promised Land and enjoy peace and prosperity during the reign of Kings David and Solomon. This was the high point for Israel—they were God's people in God's place, under God's rule, enjoying God's blessing. But the promises to Abraham had not been completely fulfilled. The problem was sin. Israel continually disobeyed God and neglected the plight of the nations. Their stubborn disobedience soon led to the demise of the partial kingdom as Israel was divided.

The prophesied kingdom. After the death of Solomon, civil war broke out and the kingdom was divided—Israel in the north and Judah in the south. After 200 years of separate existence, the northern kingdom was destroyed by the Assyrians. The southern kingdom limped on for another century and then it was captured and the people were taken exile in Babylon. During this depressing period, God spoke to the people of Israel and Judah through prophets. God explained that they were being punished for their sin, but He offered hope for a future kingdom. The prophets pointed expectantly to a time when God would send His Messiah to fulfill all His promises. The Old Testament ends waiting for God's King to appear and introduce His kingdom.

The New Testament

The present kingdom. Four hundred years of silence followed the promises of Malachi, the last of the Old Testament prophets. John the Baptist heralded the coming of the Kingdom and Jesus began His public ministry with the words, "The time has come… the kingdom of God is near" (Mark 1:15). The time of waiting was past. God's King had come to establish God's kingdom. Jesus' life and teaching proved that He was the promised King. Yet the King chose a surprising way of establishing God's kingdom—death on the cross. By His death, Jesus dealt with the problem of sin and made it possible for human beings to live in relationship with His Father. The resurrection demonstrated the success of Jesus' mission and declared hope for the world.

The proclaimed kingdom. The death and resurrection of the King accomplished everything necessary to completely restore God's kingdom. However, He did not complete the task during His earthly ministry. He ascended into heaven, indicating there would be a delay before His triumphant return. The delay provided time for all peoples to the ends of the earth to have the opportunity to hear the good news of Christ so they can live under His rule and reign. This period of the "last days" began with Pentecost when God sent His Spirit to empower and equip His church to complete the task of taking His message to the ends of the earth. This story of the advance of the kingdom continues with us, His church, today.

The perfected kingdom. One day Christ will return as the triumphant King. There will be a final division. His enemies will be separated from His presence and His rule as they are cast into hell. But His people will join Him in a perfect new creation. Revelation, the final book of the Bible, describes a fully restored kingdom where God's people from all nations will be in God's place, under His rule, enjoying His blessing forever. (Taken from *God's Big Picture* by Vaughn Roberts.)

Helps for Effective Bible Study

One of the best ways to teach someone to study the Bible is to study it with them; explaining the various tools for Bible study as you employ them. Choose a book that is meaningful to you. Another option is to start with the Gospel of John since it presents a clear picture of the person of Jesus and thus will help provide reassurance to a new believer. Once again you can use your own discretion as you ask the Holy Spirit to guide you. It is helpful to meet with your friend as often as is possible, but you can meet via the phone or email when necessary.

In the beginning, you may want to explain that there are different styles of reading, each of which has its place. Devotional or inspirational reading is often brief and provides a helpful "snack," but cannot replace in-depth study which provides the "balanced meal" necessary for spiritual growth. You may want to introduce your friend to a devotional guide that has been helpful to you. Any time one reads the Bible he should prepare to hear from God. Ask the Holy Spirit to be your teacher and guide you into understanding. Practice this each time you study the Bible with your friend. You can also read the Bible through for an overall picture. There are various plans which make this seemingly impossible task quite manageable. (See splashinfo.com for suggested reading plans.)

When you have selected a book for study, agree on how much you will attempt to read and study together. I suggest that you begin with a small section of Scripture and increase the amount over time. If you are studying the Gospel of John, you might suggest that you look at one chapter for the first week. You can instruct your friend to read the first chapter each day asking God to help with understanding. Provide several questions to help your friend read with comprehension.

- Who wrote this book?
- Who was the original intended audience?
- What do you think these verses meant to the intended audience?
- If you can, seek to determine the original context of the writing? Why was this particular text written?
- Was there anything I didn't understand? What?
- How does this passage apply to my life?
- What did God teach me? Is there a truth I need to apply? Is there a sin I need to avoid?
- How will I apply these biblical truths to my life today?
- Is there a verse I plan to memorize?

Review these questions and any others that you have found helpful when you have the opportunity to meet together. You may also suggest that as your friend reads a passage he attempts to find a key verse or write a title for the passage. It is sometimes helpful to encourage your friend to put a key passage into their own words. Suggest that he purchase a notebook and record any insights or questions he has as he studies God's Word.

As your time together progresses, you can teach your friend the importance of the two "M's"—meditation and memorization. Point him to a passage such as Joshua 1:8. "This book of the law shall not depart from your mouth, but you shall meditate on it day and night, so that you may be careful to do according to all that is written in it; for then you will make your way prosperous, and then you will have success."

You have probably already surmised that you shouldn't cover all the material in this section in one meeting. Let these principles emerge naturally from your conversation as you meet together and talk about God's Word. I promise that you will receive far more from this process than you will ever give. Just enjoy the journey.

Suggestions

Pray with your friend each time you meet.

Choose several key verses from this chapter for memorization.

Help him purchase a Bible if necessary.

Encourage him to record his insights in a notebook.

CHAPTER 2

PRAYER

How do I teach someone to pray? Good question on several levels. You may be like many Christians who struggle in their own prayer life. Therefore you don't feel qualified to teach someone else to pray. Perhaps you think that prayer is so personal and intimate that it is difficult to teach another person how to pray. You may struggle to pray in public and are wondering how you will assist another person to pray if it requires that you model prayer. These are all good questions and real concerns, but they do not absolve us from the responsibility to help our friend learn to converse with their Father.

Once again I remind you that your honesty will help your friend as they develop greater effectiveness in their prayer life. Teaching someone to pray has an added benefit—it will improve your personal prayer life.

The Priority of Jesus

It may help you to look at the prayer life of Jesus. Two passages that have helped me to understand the priority of prayer in the life of Jesus occur at the beginning and the end of His earthly ministry.

The first is found in Mark chapter one. Mark's gospel is action oriented. One of Mark's favorite words is "immediately." I am drawn to Mark's gospel because I am a very active person. Truthfully, I sometimes struggle with prayer because I view it as being passive. "It is something to do when you have exhausted all other solutions!" Yet, this event in Mark's "activity oriented" gospel helps me to understand that prayer was a priority "activity" of Jesus and thus must also be a priority for anyone who would become a fully committed follower of Christ.

Jesus begins His preaching ministry in Galilee and selects His first disciples. Their response?— "Immediately they left their nets and followed Him" (1:18). Jesus takes His disciples with Him as He enters Capernaum and teaches in the synagogue. If His teaching leaves the crowd amazed, His ability to command unclean spirits stuns them. The reaction?— "Immediately the news about Him spread everywhere into all the surrounding district of Galilee" (1:28). Clearly the word about Jesus is spreading.

When Jesus and His disciples leave the synagogue they enter the house of Simon and Andrew. Simon's mother-in-law, who is sick, is healed by Jesus. Word of the healing spreads and soon townspeople bring the sick and demon-possessed to Jesus. Mark tells us— "And the whole city had gathered at the door" (1:33). Apparently Jesus healed many of the sick; ministering until night.

When the next day dawns, the crowd has reassembled in such numbers that the disciples declare to Jesus, "Everyone is looking for You" (1:37b). It is possible that a note of reproach can be heard in their declaration. Here's my paraphrase of the encounter. "You have an opportunity to meet needs and make a name for Yourself, what are You doing out here alone?" Jesus' response to their greeting must have been surprising. "Let us go somewhere else to the towns nearby, so that I may preach there also; for that is what I came for" (1:38).

Sorry, I failed to mention what Jesus was doing early in the morning which caused the disciples to search for Him. "In the early morning, while it was still dark, Jesus got up, left the house and went away to a secluded place, and was praying there" (1:35). Prayer was the norm for Jesus. Prayer was His first priority. Prayer enabled Him to know the purpose of the Father for His life and His day. Thus His decision to focus on preaching the gospel, when so many needs begged for His attention, was made clear as He conversed with His Father.

Near the end of His earthly ministry, we find Jesus alone in the Garden of Gethsemane. Jesus had just celebrated the Passover with His disciples. He had told the disciples that one of them would betray Him. Further, He spoke of His own death which would be the sacrifice to provide for the forgiveness of sin. Nonetheless, the coming events will be so intense that all His disciples will fall away and be scattered.

Preparing for the events to come, Jesus allowed His disciples to follow as He went into the garden at

Gethsemane to pray. He confessed to His disciples that His soul was deeply grieved. He prayed with deep passion that this cup (His sacrificial death) might pass from Him. Nonetheless, He desired that the Father accomplish His will through His life. We see the intensity and honesty of Jesus' conversation with the Father along with His desire to accomplish the Father's will (Matthew 26:26-41). These two bookends of prayer show us the priority that prayer had in the life and ministry of Jesus.

If Jesus found that prayer was essential for carrying out the Father's will, we cannot neglect prayer and accomplish God's purpose. Prayer is the very breath of the Christian life and thus cannot be ignored if we are to follow Him.

Questions to Ask

You don't need to wait until you have finished the instruction on studying the Bible before you begin to talk about prayer. The *SPLASH Discipleship* outline is merely a helpful guideline. You will discover that prayer and Bible study flow together naturally. When you meet or talk on the phone about the process of spiritual growth, you will want to pray for and with your friend. As you pray, you will be "showing" or modeling how to pray. Don't let that idea frighten you. You want to demonstrate and teach the truth that prayer is simply *conversing with God in one's own language and thoughts.*

A couple of simple questions may help you to know how best to begin. Ask, "What do you know about prayer?" "Have you ever tried to pray?" "Tell me about your experience with prayer?" "Now that you have accepted Christ as your personal Savior, have you sensed anything different as you pray?"

Prayer is Simply Conversation with Your Father

When Jesus taught His disciples how to pray, He indicated that they could address God as "Abba" Father. "Abba" is a term of endearment; it indicates a personal and intimate relationship.

The great apostle Paul indicated that his prayer life was radically altered by his personal relationship with Christ. In Romans chapter 8 Paul discusses the spiritual life inaugurated by the Spirit. He speaks of the spiritual victory believers can experience as we live by the Spirit. "For you have not received a spirit of slavery leading to fear again, but you have received a spirit of adoption as sons by which we cry out, 'Abba! Father!'" (8:15). First century Jews prayed regularly, but most prayed out of a sense of religious duty. Believers pray from a sense of gratitude to a Father who has redeemed and adopted us. It is a privileged conversation between a child and his heavenly Father.

I have three daughters whom I dearly love. Nothing brings me greater joy than talking to them in person or on the phone. What do we talk about? We talk about life. We talk about their fears and failures as well as their accomplishments. They tell me about the mundane things that make up their daily lives. They tell me they love me and appreciate all I do for them. I love to hear their messages of gratitude. My girls and I enjoy regular conversations about any and every aspect of life. It may help you to think about this parental image and remember that the Father enjoys His time with you and loves to give His children good gifts (Matthew 7:11).

Prayer is nothing more than a child conversing with his loving Father. You can talk to Him about anything. Use your regular voice and vocabulary. You don't have to use "Bible language" or a "preacher's voice" to talk to God. As you guide your friend in prayer you can tell him these truths, but you can also demonstrate these truths as you pray for him and with him. The more honest and simple you are as you pray, the better your friend will learn to enjoy talking to his Father.

Every conversation involves talking and listening. We often focus on the "talking" aspect of prayer and forget to mention "listening." We most often hear God speak to us through His written word, the Bible. This means that we should link prayer and Bible study. Pray before you begin to read the Bible and pray as you read it, asking God to speak to you. As we read and meditate on Scripture, we can hear God speak to us. He will often prompt us by reminding us of a text or event in our lives. Practice "listening to God" with your friend. You might ask, "What did you hear God saying to you as we prayed together or as we read the Bible today?"

Pray in Jesus' Name

We pray to God the Father, but we do so in Jesus' name. When Jesus was preparing His disciples for His earthly departure, He told them that they would soon be able to address the Father in His name. "Whatever you ask in My name, that will I do, so that the Father may be glorified in the Son. If you ask Me anything in My name, I will do it" (John 14:13-14).

Your friend may wonder what it means to pray in Jesus' name. It is more than simply "affixing His name" to the end of our prayers. It means first, that we are praying based on the personal relationship we have with the Son. In John 14:6 Jesus told His disciples that He alone was the way, the truth, and the life, and that no one had access to the Father, except through Him. Thus to pray in Jesus name indicates that we have a personal relationship with God through Christ and intimate access to the Father.

To pray in Jesus' name also indicates that we pray according to His character. In other words, we pray in such a manner that our requests advance His kingdom and accomplish His will. The promise that we can ask "anything" is not a "name it-claim it" promise as if we can manipulate God through our prayers. As God's children, His desires become our desires and thus our requests will be in accord with the character and mission of Christ.

Using the Lord's Prayer as a Model

When Jesus' disciples asked Him to teach them to pray, He responded with what we call the Lord's Prayer. It is found in several different forms. The most familiar is in Matthew 6:9-13. This is a good text to look at as you talk about prayer. Jesus did not mean for His disciples to simply recite it as a sort of "religious mantra." Rather, He intended them to use it as a framework for conversing with God throughout the day.

In the discussion that precedes this prayer, Jesus indicates that His disciples should pray to receive the reward of His Father rather than that of man. Further, He indicates that an all-knowing God does not need information. "For your Father knows what you need before you ask Him" (6:8). Thus our prayer does not "inform" God, rather it "adores" God. The reward of the Father is His presence, His provision, and His protection. These blessings we celebrate in prayer. When we long for the presence of God, we will be inextricably drawn to prayer.

The address "our Father" indicates the personal nature of prayer for the follower of Christ. Prayer is family conversation. The phrase, "Who art in heaven," does not suggest that God is "far off" and "unapproachable." Rather, it underlines His majesty and sovereignty. We pray to God who is worthy of all praise and is able to answer prayer.

The declaration "hallowed be Your Name" should remind us to praise God simply because He is worthy of praise. Further the statement "hallowed be Your name" should remind us that as "Christians" we now bear the name of "Christ" and thus we are requesting that He manifest His character in us. The study of this text is an appropriate time to begin to talk about the transformed life which the Holy Spirit will manifest in the believer enabling him to clearly reflect God's character.

"Your kingdom come, Your will be done, on earth as it is in heaven" reminds us that the purpose of our life is to advance His kingdom. Prayer is not about "us" it is about "God." We are asking God to help us see the world from His point of view and advance His kingdom through our actions and words. We are committing to live with immediate and unconditional obedience.

The requests for daily bread, forgiveness of sins, and victory over evil cover everything the disciple needs to be an effective follower of Christ. Daily bread relates to all the necessities of life. Teach your friend that he can talk with the Father about anything and everything. Nothing is too small or insignificant for the Father's attention when it comes to His children. The mention of forgiveness reminds us to constantly confess our sins and accept God's forgiveness as we forgive others. We seek God's guidance throughout the day as we seek to live above temptation.

Finally, we acknowledge that our purpose is to advance His kingdom by His power and for His glory. This prayer provides a framework for our constant awareness of God's presence, provision, and protection as we seek first His kingdom and His righteousness (Matthew 6:33). Throughout the day, you can think through the various aspects of this prayer as you practice the presence of Christ. For further study on the Lord's Prayer, you might want to purchase *The Prayer of Jesus* by Ken Hemphill (Broadman and Holman).

Use the Acrostic ACTS

It is sometimes helpful to use an acrostic to keep us focused as we pray. One of the classic ones on prayer is **ACTS** which stands for Adoration, Confession, Thanksgiving, and Supplication. You can use this to aid your friend as he grows in his prayer life. Practice the **ACTS** outline as you pray together.

Adoration means that it is appropriate to enter the King's presence with praise. Suggest that one way to praise God is to reflect on His attributes such as His holiness, goodness, patience etc. You can also praise Him as you reflect on His names and His mighty deeds. You may want to choose some of the Psalms and use those to voice your praise to God. It is always helpful to pray Scripture. Here are a few Psalms to get you started.

Psalm 23

Psalm 51

Psalm 67

Psalm 69:13-31

Psalm 71:17-23

Psalm 93

Confession simply means that we agree with God about our sin. Remember God knows everything and thus confession does not reveal to God anything about us that He doesn't already know. John speaks about the importance of confession in his first letter. "If we confess our sins, He is faithful and righteous to forgive us our sins and to cleanse us from all unrighteousness" (1 John 1:9). That verse contains an incredible promise —we can receive forgiveness and cleansing from the Father! We need to be as specific in confessing our sin as we were in committing the sin.

By the way, John also speaks about the lack of confession. "If we say that we have not sinned, we make Him a liar and His word is not in us" (1 John 1:10). He follows this warning with a reminder that children should never desire to sin, but that when they do sin, they can be assured they have an advocate with the Father. Our advocate? Jesus Christ who is righteous. This truth should give us great confidence as we confess our sins.

Thanksgiving is the characteristic of the Christian who recognizes that everything comes from the hand of the Father. "Let us come before His presence with thanksgiving, let us shout joyfully to Him with psalms" (Psalm 95:2). As you pray together, thank God for all that He has done for you throughout the day. Thanksgiving allows us to count our blessings. Thanksgiving is one of the characteristics of the believer. Unbelievers do not honor God as God and thus do not give thanks (Romans 1:21).

Supplication is the act of bringing your requests before God. "Be anxious for nothing, but in everything by prayer and supplication with thanksgiving let your requests be made known to God" (Philippians 4:6). As a child of God, you have the privilege of bringing all your requests to the Father. Remember, prayer in Jesus' name is never self-centered and thus you should teach your friend to pray for others. Teach them how to make a prayer list and watch for God to answer requests.

Link Prayer and Bible Study

Prayer and Bible study are like twins. Prayer should always accompany our study of God's Word. Prayer prepares the mind to understand God's Word and the heart to obey it. Further, it allows us to respond to what God says to us. Meditation on Scripture is one means of hearing God speak to us.

Meditation allows the Holy Spirit to transform knowledge *about God* into knowledge *of God.* It moves us from information to transformation. Meditation is not clearing our mind of all conscious thoughts. It is focusing our mind on the truths of God. Thus we call to mind, think over, and dwell on the things we hear as God speaks to us in His Word. Meditation is to ruminate over the truths of God about His character, His works, His purposes, and His promises.

Prayer Promises that Encourage Us to Pray

- Psalm 6:9 "The Lord has heard my supplication, The Lord receives my prayer."

- Proverbs 15:29 "The Lord is far from the wicked, but He hears the prayer of the righteous."

- Matthew 7:7 "Ask, and it will be given to you; seek, and you will find; knock, and it will be opened to you."

- Matthew 7:11 "If you then, being evil, know how to give good gifts to your children, how much more will your Father who is in heaven give what is good to those who ask Him?"

- Philippians 4:6-7 "Be anxious for nothing, but in everything by prayer and supplication with thanksgiving let your requests be made know to God. And the peace of God, which surpasses all comprehension, will guard your hearts and your minds in Christ Jesus."

- I Thessalonians 5:16-18 "Rejoice always; pray without ceasing; in everything give thanks; for this is God's will for you in Christ Jesus."

- James 1:5 "But if any of you lacks wisdom, let him ask of God, who gives to all generously and without reproach, and it will be given to him."

- James 5:16 "Therefore, confess your sins to one another, and pray for one another so that you may be healed. The effective prayer of a righteous man can accomplish much."

Suggestions

Make Scripture memory cards for several of the verses above and memorize them together.

Memorize the Lord's Prayer and use it as an outline for praying without ceasing.

Start a prayer journal.

CHAPTER 3

LOVE

LOVE GOD—LOVE YOUR NEIGHBOR

As you assist your friend to grow in his Christian walk, you will want to keep it simple. You may be wondering how anyone can communicate the essence of Christianity. We would be wise to follow the leadership of the Master discipler.

A scribe, an expert on the law, asked Jesus "What commandment is the foremost of all?" (Mark 12:28). Jesus, understanding His audience, quotes the Shema, the ancient Jewish confession of faith. "Jesus answered, 'The foremost is, "Hear, O Israel! The Lord our God is one Lord; and you shall love the Lord Your God with all your heart, and with all your soul, and with all your mind, and with all your strength." 'The second is this, "You shall love your neighbor as yourself." 'There is no other commandment greater than these'" (Mark 12:30-31). If this definition of committed discipleship was sufficient for our Lord, it should be good enough for us.

Christianity is a love affair with God that grows in depth, intensity, and beauty as we learn more about

Him. A simple definition of what it means to be a growing Christian is to give all you know about yourself at any one time to all that you know about God at that same time. As we grow in our understanding of ourselves and of God, our love affair with God will grow.

God Wants All of You

Some new believers think that they can add the Christian commitment to their already crowded life in the same way they might add another line to their resume. Remember, Jesus warned that man cannot serve two masters for he will love the one and hate the other (Matthew 6:24). He was warning about the attempt to love God and love the world at the same time. The whole person is the object of God's covenant love and thus the whole man is claimed by God for Himself. The Christian seeks God with a passionate single-mindedness out of gratitude for the knowledge that while we were sinners, Christ died for the ungodly (Romans 5:8).

God doesn't save only a portion of us and therefore we cannot offer Him only a portion of ourselves. To love God with all our being determines the disposition of our lives including our thoughts, actions, activities, and passions. This love requires us to place our entire self at God's disposal.

When we attempt to compartmentalize our lives, giving God only a portion, we will suffer from religious schizophrenia. We can't serve Him one day of the week and ignore Him the other six. We can't praise Him at church on Sunday and ignore His principles by living our daily lives as if God does not care about our work, our play, and our interpersonal relationships.

Here's how Paul states the principle of loving God with one's total being. "Therefore I urge you, brethren, by the mercies of God, to present your bodies a living and holy sacrifice, acceptable to God, which is your spiritual service of worship. And do not be conformed to this world, but be transformed by the renewing of your mind, so that you may prove what the will of God is, that which is good and acceptable and perfect" (Romans 12:1-2). It is the presentation of one's entire being to God which creates the platform for the transformation of our mind and thus our ability to know and accomplish the will of God.

Notice that the presentation of our bodies is our "spiritual service of worship." The word "spiritual" can also be translated as "logical." It is the service which logically follows the understanding that in redemption we have received the mercies of God. In other words, this is normal Christianity.

"This world" refers to the influences of the world as set against the things of God. The forces of the world want to squeeze us into the mold of the world. The pressures and passions of the world appeal to the "old man" or the "old nature." When we receive Christ, we become new creatures (2 Corinthians 5:17) but we still must deal with the old sin nature. The good news is that we can stand against the pressures of the world as we are transformed by the renewing of our minds. This transforming process occurs as the indwelling Holy Spirit teaches us the truths of God's Word and produces in us the fruit of the Spirit (Galatians 5:22-24).

41

The transformation of the mind occurs as we present ourselves fully to God. By the way, did you notice that God has already declared the gift of our bodies to be good, acceptable, and perfect? When you give yourself to God, He is pleased.

It would be helpful to study Romans 12:1-2 and 2 Corinthians 5:17 with your friend. Explain what it means to be a new person in Christ and how the transformation occurs as we study and obey God's Word. Our spiritual growth is a lifelong process and will enable us to overcome the temptations of the flesh and the allures of the world.

Love God with All Your Heart

When the Bible speaks of the "heart" it is talking about the very center of one's being, the command center of life. It is the place that controls our feelings, emotions, desires, and passions. It is the place where religious commitment is established and consequently, the new creation begins in the heart. Ezekiel, the Old Testament prophet, talks about removing a heart of stone and replacing it with a heart of flesh which desires to respond to the word of God (Ezekiel 11:19-20). He then contrasts the new heart that longs for God and His word with the old one that goes after detestable things and abominations (21). When we are saved, we receive this new heart. In truth, we become new creatures. The Holy Spirit now indwells us enabling us to love God with all our heart.

We see a very similar idea in the teaching of Jesus as recorded in Mark 7:21-23. "For from within, out of the heart of men, proceed the evil thoughts, fornications, thefts, murders, adulteries, deeds of coveting and wickedness, as well as deceit, sensuality, envy, slander, pride and foolishness. All these things proceed from within and defile the man." The unconverted heart is both wicked and easily deceived.

Jesus condemned the Pharisees by quoting Isaiah. "This people honors me with their lips, but their heart is far away from me" (Mark 7:6). The Pharisees said all the right things, but they gave God lip service not heart service. You will need to help your fellow traveler understand that Christianity is not merely about the right confession; it is about a passionate love affair of the heart that changes every aspect of one's life. Explain to your new Christian friend that when he received Christ, he became a new creature. "Therefore if anyone is in Christ, he is a new creature; the old things passed away; behold, new things have come" (2 Corinthians 5:17). Christians have received a new heart that desires God and has the capacity to obey His word.

Jesus clearly taught that one's treasure will determine the passion of one's heart (Matthew 6:21). The treasure of our heart is God alone. To love God will all our heart means to place Him at the center of every aspect of our lives. We give Him our feelings, emotions, desires, and passions. When we allow the old nature to reassume control, we must confess that area of sin, turn from it, and present our heart once again to God. The giving of our heart to God should be a daily practice.

Discuss together what it means to love God with all one's heart. What impact would such a love affair with God have on my work, play, and other relationships? Is there anything or anyone who currently stands in the way of loving God with all my heart?

Love God with All Your Soul

In the creation narrative, we are told that God breathed into man the breath of life and he became a living "soul" or living "being" (Genesis 2:7). Soul refers to the animating force of life; the vital essence of man. The indication that man is body, soul, and spirit does not mean he can be divided up into component parts. Together they describe the various aspects of the inseparable whole person that must be presented to God. We will see places of overlap as we discuss what it means to love God with all your heart, your soul, your mind, and your strength.

"Soul" can be used to refer to the entire human being in its physical life thus requiring food and clothing. In Matthew 6:25 Jesus told the disciples they did not need to be worried about their "soul" or "life" concerning what they will eat or drink. The cure for such earthly anxiety? There are two parts—the sure knowledge that our Father knows our needs and desires to meet them (Matthew 6:32) and our commitment to seek first the kingdom of God and His righteousness (6:33). When we love God with all our soul it means that we love Him with our physical lives which includes all the stuff of our life such as food, clothing, money, time, and talents.

Sometimes the word "soul" is used to denote the feelings, wishes, and will of man. The soul can desire evil (Proverbs 21:10), but it can also seek after God

(Psalm 42:2-3). The soul has a range of emotions so that it can be spoken of as being incited, embittered, confirmed, unsettled, or kept in suspense. The Bible speaks of the bitter soul of the childless, the sick, or the threatened. The soul can also express positive emotions. It rejoices, praises, hopes, and is patient.

Thus, loving God with our soul means we surrender to Him our emotions. We confess and turn from those bitter emotions and give Him our joy, praise, and hope. Discuss issues such as bitterness or an unforgiving spirit which can keep one from loving God with all one's soul. Lead your friend in confession followed by praise.

Love God with All Your Mind

The mind allows us to think, perceive, and reflect. It directs our opinions and judgments. While our love of God certainly involves an emotional response, it also requires that we respond with our intellect. Tragically, many Christians live most of their Christian life in the realm of feeling with little commitment to the command to love God with their mind.

Peter instructs the believer to "Sanctify Christ as Lord in your hearts, always being ready to make a defense to everyone who asks you to give an account for the hope that is in you, yet with gentleness and reverence" (1 Peter 3:15). Did you notice the linking of the heart and the mind in this passage? To sanctify Christ as Lord in our hearts requires that we prepare our minds which, in turn, will enable us to explain the hope we have in Christ. Congratulations, working through this book is evidence that you are willing to love God with all your mind.

Paul exhorts young Timothy, "Be diligent to present yourself approved to God as a workman who does not need to be ashamed, accurately handling the word of truth" (2 Timothy 2:15). Loving God with all our mind requires that we read and study God's Word along with other good books. Reading and studying should be a delight and a life-long process for the believer who wants to love God with their total being. Our desire to please God and know Him more completely should lead to a lifelong commitment to learning.

But loving God with our entire mind also means that we learn to see the world from God's viewpoint. We need to develop a Christian world-view or lens through which we view the world. In the Christian world-view the Bible becomes the standard by which we evaluate all of life. Loving God with our entire mind should therefore impact our thinking and our response to every area of human existence.

Many Christians remain stunted because they fail to love God with all their minds. You will want to assist your friend to develop a passion for life-long learning. Help your friend develop a plan for reading the Bible and other good Christian material on a consistent basis. Share a Christian book that you have read recently. Coach him as he reads through the book. Explain those areas that he finds confusing. You will learn and grow together as you are obedient to love God with your entire mind.

At this juncture, it will be helpful to assist your friend in building a library with several essential tools to assist in Bible study, such as a Bible dictionary, a good one-volume commentary, and a Bible atlas. You will find some suggestions on splashinfo.com.

Love God with All Your Strength

Strength refers to all our physical capacities. You will recall that we have already looked at Romans 12:1 where Paul instructs us to present our "bodies" as a living sacrifice. When we present our physical bodies to God we are presenting our all our gifts and abilities since they reside in our physical bodies.

The presentation of our bodies as part of our commitment to love God with all our strength mandates that we learn to serve God. To love God with all our strength indicates an "all out" commitment to service. This command calls to my mind the Olympic athlete who trains diligently and strains with all intensity to compete at the highest level for a brief moment in time and a perishable reward. Our service enables us to lay up treasure in heaven, treasures that are imperishable (Matthew 6:19-20).

The apostle Paul uses similar athletic imagery to talk about the intensity of his service to the Lord. In 1 Corinthians 9:24-27 he speaks of running to win the race. He writes of exercising self-control and disciplining his body so that his work will not be disqualified. Don't lower the bar when it comes to talking to your friend about what it means to be a Christian. God gave His best and we must be willing to do the same. Our love for God demands all our strength.

This may be an appropriate time to talk about serving God through His community—the church.

Share ideas from your own life and indicate how you have given God the strength of your life. Take your friend with you to observe you as you participate in some area of service. Often a visible example is all it takes to teach this principle. Once again, you might pose the question, "Is there anything that keeps you from serving God with all your strength?"

Love Your Neighbor as Yourself

Christianity, by its very definition, is a community affair. We cannot love God whom we have not seen and not love our brother whom we have seen (cf. 1 John 4:20). Loving ourselves as one created in God's image and redeemed by God's grace mandates that we love all other persons created in God's image. The fact that we received grace when it was undeserved enables us to show grace to others. The parable of the Good Samaritan (Luke 10:25-37) tells us that our "neighbor" may include persons we don't know and don't necessarily like. There is no "non-neighbor." Anyone who needs me is my neighbor.

You might want to study 1 John 3:13-22 and 4:7-21 with your friend. Point out that love is not an emotional attachment, it is active goodwill. "Little children, let us not love with word or with tongue, but in deed and truth" (1 John 3:18). If the two of you have already identified a "neighbor" in need, talk about an act of love you can do for that neighbor.

When you look at the church in the book of Acts, you will see an amazing picture of "loving one's neighbor." The early Christians not only enjoyed meeting with each other from house to house, when they saw a need, they responded by selling property and possessions and sharing with those in need (Acts 4:32-35). Can you think of a ministry project you can do together to meet the need of someone in your community?

We will talk about the need for fellowship with other believers when we discuss accountability, but it is appropriate to begin to introduce this concept now as you dialogue about loving God and loving one's neighbor.

One way that you can practice "loving your neighbor" with a new believer is to ask them if they are holding a grudge against anyone. Suggest that they actively release that person by asking God to forgive them and then to go to that person and seek forgiveness and restitution. You might also ask them if they know someone who needs to understand the gift of forgiveness and redemption they have recently received. Offer to go with them and help them to share their story. You can explain this is what you did when you shared with them.

Suggestions

We have looked at several significant verses in this chapter. Here is a partial listing. Pick a few for memorization.

Matthew 6:21

Matthew 6:33

Romans 12:1-2

2 Corinthians 5:17
Galatians 5:22-23
2 Timothy 2:15
I John 4:20

Take a trip to a local Christian bookstore and help your friend start a good Christian library.

Participate in a ministry outing together.

Accompany your friend as he tells someone else about his commitment to Christ.

A DISCIPLER'S GUIDE

CHAPTER 4

ACCOUNTABILITY

Throughout the process of *splashing* your friend to Christ, you have been emphasizing personal relationship over *religious activity.* We are now moving into the area of accountability in a community of believers which brings into focus one's need for fellowship with a local body of believers—a church.

This means that you will have to help your friend understand the difference between personal involvement in a church as the natural outworking of one's personal relationship with Christ and church membership as a religious activity earning one merit. Many people, when asked about their personal relationship with Christ, will answer by telling you the name of the church or denomination to which they belong. They have confused personal relationship with church membership.

You should not encounter a significant problem here because you have been consistent throughout the discipling process to talk about the need for and joy of a personal relationship with God through Jesus Christ.

The issue of accountability will allow you to talk about the ongoing need that every believer has for community. You have a ready illustration of accountability and that is the personal relationship that has already been forged between the two of you. Explain that one's relationship with a New Testament church will enlarge the circle of friendship and provide a place of effective service. We began to talk about service in our last section when we discussed loving God with all one's strength.

This discussion will lead naturally to the topic of stewardship which includes one's time, talents, testimony, and treasure. We will cover that next, but remember this book simply provides guidelines and helps. Feel free to move from topic to topic as the need presents itself and the Spirit guides. This may be new to you, but I have every confidence that you can do this with the power of the Spirit.

Helpful Questions

Once again we want our discipling process to be personal and conversational. It should be the most natural thing in the world for two believers who share a personal relationship with Christ.

You will find it helpful at this point to find out what your friend knows about the church and what experiences, if any, they have had when attending church. Their recollections may be simply "warm" childhood memories or they may be negative experiences of liberalism or legalism. You will want to know what they have experienced so you can customize your discussion to help them understand the dynamic potential of a true covenant community of born again believers in relationship with Christ and one another for the advance of the kingdom through the redemption of the nations.

I know that last sentence is a long one, but it is actually a good definition of what the church is all about. Look at it again. I want you to be able to communicate with genuine enthusiasm that our relationship with an authentic New Testament church provides us the forum for "living with eternal impact."

I suggest you ask several leading questions. You do not need to ask all of them since some will clearly overlap. From the personal relationship you have established through the entire *SPLASH* process, you may already know much of this information. Use any of these at your discretion.

"Do you attend any church now?" If so, *"Where do you attend?"* *"What has been your experience there?"* *"What do you like most about it?"* If you discover they do not attend church, you will want to find out about past experiences. *"Have you attended church in the past?"* *"Which one and what did you think?"* *"What do you think is the purpose of the church?"* *"Do you think it has any connection to your personal experience with Christ?"*

You are certainly free to ask other questions that will help determine any misconceptions or fears you may have to overcome in helping your friend establish a vital connection to a community of believers. Most likely you will want to introduce them to your church family and small group. This will be a natural connection since you can attend with them and help them understand

what they are seeing and experiencing. Tell them that
you will sit with them and explain anything they don't
understand. Go to lunch after church and continue the
dialogue about the morning's experience.

It is also possible that they are presently attending
a church and you may simply need to help them fully
understand how church involvement can enhance
their personal relationship with Christ. You may need
to attend with them so you can understand what
their church is like and what they believe. You want
your friend to enjoy the fellowship of a church that
accurately teaches the Bible and is committed to the
great commission.

Created for Fellowship

One of the first statements God makes about
man after creation is that it is not good for man to be
alone (Genesis 2:18). You know that the context goes
on to talk about marriage and one's personal helper.
Nonetheless, the principle is true and clear throughout
Scripture. Man is created to enjoy a relationship with
God and with man who is created in God's image.

The first letter of John has much to say about man's
need for fellowship. In the first three verses of the first
chapter, John talks about the early believers' personal
encounter with Christ. Now listen to verses 3 and
4—"What we have seen and heard we proclaim to you
also, so that you too may have fellowship with us; and
indeed our fellowship is with the Father, and with His
Son Jesus Christ. These things we write, so that our joy
may be made complete" (1 John 1:3-4).

Did you notice the inextricable relationship between fellowship with the Father and the Son and relationship with other believers? Further, John indicates that he is writing this letter so that "our joy may be made complete." As the gospel is shared and others come to Christ and to His community, joy is expanded. When someone remains outside of Christ and His community, our joy and our fellowship are lacking.

Later in chapter three John compares Christ's love for us with our love for the brethren. "We know love by this, that He laid down His life for us; and we ought to lay down our lives for the brethren" (16). John continues the theme of fellowship by talking about sharing of our goods with brothers in need and indicates that intimacy of fellowship will give us confidence before God. He then cites a commandment from God—"This is His commandment, that we believe in the name of His Son Jesus Christ, and love one another, just as He commanded us" (23). Notice again the connection between believing in Jesus and loving one another.

In chapter four, John once again connects loving God with loving others. "Beloved, let us love one another, for love is from God; and everyone who loves is born of God and knows God. The one who does not love does not know God" (7-8). John leaves little room for misunderstanding—"If someone says, 'I love God,' and hates his brother, he is a liar; for the one who does not love his brother whom he has seen, cannot love God whom he has not seen. And this commandment we have from Him, that the one who loves God should love his brother also" (20-21).

The book of Hebrews was written when persecution of the early church had become intense. It contains several passages which underline the importance of standing firm in the faith together. Read Hebrews 10:19-25. This passage begins with the affirmation that we have been given personal access to God through our experience of salvation (19-20). This affirmation is followed by three statements that begin with the phrase "let us"—let us draw near in full assurance (22), let us hold fast the confession (23), and let us consider how to stimulate one anther to love and good deeds (24). Notice that these three commands are based on our commitment to assemble together with other believers. "Not forsaking our own assembling together, as is the habit of some, but encouraging one another; and all the more as you see the day drawing near" (25).

When we accept Christ, we are born into a family of fellow-believers, and we express our family connection as we learn to live and love in community. Share your story concerning how you came to establish a relationship with other believers through your church family. Be open and honest about fears and failures as well as joys and successes.

Jesus and His Church

The first use of the word "church" by Jesus occurs in Matthew 16:18—"I also say to you that you are Peter, and upon this rock I will build My church; and the gates of Hades will not overpower it." Open your Bible to that passage and read it in its entirety.

Speculation about the identity of Jesus was growing in intensity. People had recognized that He was no ordinary man and that His teaching contained a different level of authority than the traditional rabbis of their day. They were identifying Jesus with the Old Testament prophets. You may recall that prophecy in Israel had ceased after the message of Malachi nearly four hundred years earlier.

Jesus used the growing interest in His identity to ask the disciples what they had concluded concerning His identity. Peter, the spokesman for the twelve, answered that they had come to believe that He is the Christ, the Son of the living God. Jesus confirmed His identity and further indicated that this knowledge was given them by the Father. It is at this critical juncture of revelation that Jesus made known to His disciples His plan to build His church.

It is important to notice the inter-relatedness of Christ and His church. His mission on earth then and now involves the creation and empowering of His church. Again, we can define church as a covenant community of born again believers in relationship with Jesus Christ for the advance of His kingdom until all the nations have the opportunity to know Him as their rightful King. The Bible refers to the church as the Bride of Christ, the body, the field, and the building. When we come to know Christ, we will become passionate about His church.

The church is God's strategy for advancing His kingdom on earth. Paul declares that the church is empowered by the resurrection of Christ to express God's fullness on earth (Ephesians 1:18-23). He tells of the wonder he felt as an apostle when he was permitted to make known the mystery which for ages had been hidden by the Creator. "So that the manifold wisdom of God might now be made known through the church to the rulers and the authorities in the heavenly places. This was in accordance with the eternal purpose which He carried out in Christ Jesus our Lord" (Ephesians 3:10-11).

The church provides the platform for every believer's engagement in kingdom service. It allows us to invest our lives in such a manner that we can have an eternal impact. You may recall that the passage in Matthew 16 which began our discussion of Jesus and His church declared that the church has been given the keys of the kingdom. Those "keys" are the message of the King and the redemption He alone offers. Jesus promised that what is bound through the church will be bound eternally in heaven. That means that your ministry through the church has eternal consequences. Jesus promised that the gates of Hell cannot withstand the onslaught of the church. The church may sometimes seem small and impotent, but hell cannot stand against His church. We are saved and called to be part of that church.

Characteristics of a Great Church

Since church is not a divine country club, we will want to be involved in a great church, that is, an effective church. When I use the word "great" I am not referring to size or budget, I am referring to its heart for God. Here are a few things to look for in a great church.

- A great church believes and teaches the Bible. Does the pastor encourage people to follow his sermon in the Bible? Is the sermon Bible-based? Do people sitting around you have their Bible open?

- A great church takes prayer and worship seriously. Do you sense God's presence in the worship service? Does the worship leader focus your attention on God? Is prayer an integral part of the worship service? Are there other times when people gather for corporate prayer?

- A great church has a passion for the world and an active concern for the lost. Does the church have an outreach strategy? Do people in small groups pray for their lost friends? Are people regularly encouraged to bring friends to church events?

- A great church is generous about giving to others and has a strategy for reaching Jerusalem, Judea, Samaria, and the ends of the earth (Acts 1:8). What percentage of the budget is allocated for outreach? What about mission giving? Do the people seem to have enthusiasm for giving?

- A great church is cooperative in spirit, structure, and practice. Do they fellowship with other churches of like faith and practice? Do they work with others in meeting social and spiritual needs of the community?

- A great church teaches sound doctrine based on Scripture and not tradition. Ask to see the church's statement of faith.

- A great church has a genuine sense of community. Do people appear to enjoy each other's company?

Is there a sense of excitement in the hallways? Do they pray for each other's needs?

If you want to read more about the church and its biblical character you might enjoy my book *Eternal Impact: The Passion of Kingdom Centered Communities.* You could study this book with your friend. Study guides and a teaching DVD are available.

Suggestions

Attend church together and talk about what you experienced.

Work on Scripture memory from this section. A few recommended verses are:

Acts 1:8

Hebrews 10:25

1 John 1:3-4

A DISCIPLER'S GUIDE

CHAPTER 5

STEWARDSHIP

One of the most exciting concepts in all of Scripture is that of stewardship. *Steward is who we are and stewardship is what we do.* Stewardship acknowledges both God's ownership of everything and His high regard for man whom He personally placed in charge of all He owns. Under the general heading of "stewardship" we will look at five areas of life that will at times overlap. They will be easy for you to remember since they all begin with the letter "T." We are responsible for earthly stewardship of our **temple**, **time**, **talents**, **testimony**, and **treasure**.

In the beginning!

The phrase "in the beginning" that begins the story of God's revelation to man in Genesis 1:1 should not be read as a simple introductory phrase like "once upon a time." "In the beginning" has profound theological significance.

- First it indicates that everything had a beginning. The universe did not always exist;

it is not eternal. Only God is eternal and thus everything owes its existence to Him. Creation is God's gift to Himself.

- Further, "in the beginning" suggests that there is more to come. God is still at work in the world. Good news— you are part of God's continuing activity on planet earth. God created you in His image and invested great opportunity and responsibility in you. God created you personally and purposefully. God desires for you to live in dynamic relationship with Him and join Him in His ongoing earthly activity. God has chosen to accomplish His kingdom activity on earth through willing human instruments. In other words, you can live with eternal impact.

- "In the beginning" also anticipates a culmination or ultimate end. Here's how the prophet Isaiah stated it—"Remember the former things long past, For I am God, and there is no other; I am God, and there is no one like Me, declaring the end from the beginning, and from ancient times things which have not been done. Saying, 'My purpose will be established, and I will accomplish all My good pleasure'" (Isaiah 46:9-10).

It is exciting to know that you are created to be part of something that is bigger than this world and eternal in significance. Paul talks about God's ultimate plan to sum up everything in heaven and earth in Christ so that He will come to have first place in everything. Paul indicates that God will accomplish this through His church (Colossians 1:18-20). You can help your friend understand that their service through their church will have eternal consequences.

- Finally, "in the beginning" indicates that God is the owner of everything since He created it. This truth has a profound bearing on our everyday lives and our attitude toward our physical bodies, time, talents, testimony, and treasure. When we acknowledge that God is owner, we must first confess "we are not owners." If we are not owners, then what are we?

Let's go back to the Genesis account. "Then God said, 'Let Us make man in Our image, according to Our likeness; and let them rule over the fish of the sea and over the birds of the sky and over the cattle and over all the earth, and over every creeping thing that creeps on the earth" (Genesis 1:26). He then blesses man, both male and female and instructs them to multiply, fill the earth, subdue it, and rule over it. The point is clear—God created man in His image—relational, rational, and responsible—to be His stewards over all His created order.

You were created to live in relationship to God and man. You are a rational being and therefore you can understand God's Word which reveals His will for your life. This ultimately means that we will be responsible for how we use God's resources which have been placed in our stewardship.

Can you imagine having such privilege and responsibility? You were created by God and entrusted with His creation. You are a steward and as such you are responsible for all that God has placed with you in trust. Help your friend to see stewardship as a privilege and not an onerous legalism.

The overarching principle of stewardship is ultimate accountability!

When Paul wrote to the Corinthians, he had to deal with numerous problems related to spiritual pride, divisiveness in the church, and a general lack of responsible stewardship. There is a most instructive passage in 1 Corinthians 3:10-15. You should look at that passage in its context. This would be an excellent passage to study with your friend.

Paul spoke of his ministry in Corinth as foundational. He was the person who God allowed to plant the church in Corinth. Notice that he referred to his ability to build as an activity of God's grace. "Grace" (charis) is the root word found in charismata, which we translate as "spiritual gift." In other words, Paul's work was based on the stewardship of the gifts for ministry given Him by God.

Paul was writing about the roles that he and Apollos played in building the community. But in verse 12 through 15 Paul widened the scope of the discussion to include every believer. "Now if any man builds on the foundation with gold, silver, precious stones, wood, hay, straw, each man's work will become evident; for the day will show it because it is to be revealed with fire and the fire itself will test the quality of each man's work" (12-13).

We need to underline several key principles related to our topic of the stewardship of one's earthly life.

1. Every believer is a builder. Building is not an option for the believer. You were created by God with a purpose in mind and you have the privilege of fulfilling that purpose by placing your life at His disposal.

2. You do determine the materials you use to build. The building materials mentioned speak of both value and quality. Wood, hay, and straw have neither value nor quality and thus they are consumed by fire. Gold, silver, and precious stones will be refined when they are tested by fire. We should always offer our best in service to the King. Nothing else is ever appropriate.

3. We will be held accountable for all that we have been given by the King. Privilege and opportunity mandate accountability. Here is how Luke states this principle—"From everyone who has been given much, much will be required; and to whom they entrusted much, of him they will ask all the more" (Luke 12:48b).

4. Accountability means that your life matters. God holds us accountable because He values us! When you place yourself at God's disposal, He will work through you to accomplish kingdom activity.

Five areas of privilege and stewardship

Temple. Look again at the text we are considering in 1 Corinthians 3. Paul declared—"Do you not know that you are a temple of God and that the Spirit of

God dwells in you?" (1 Corinthians 3:16). Paul again employed the image of the body as a temple of God when discussing the matter of sexual purity in 1 Corinthians 6:12-20. "Or do you not know that your body is a temple of the Holy Spirit who is in you, whom you have from God, and that you are not your own? For you have been bought with a price; therefore glorify God in your body" (19-20). Now that you are a Christian, you belong to God both by creation and redemption. God paid a high price to redeem you— the sacrifice of His only begotten Son. As stewards of this great gift we are to offer our bodies to God.

Paul instructed believers in Rome to offer their bodies as a living and holy sacrifice acceptable to God as a spiritual act of worship (Romans 12:1). A living sacrifice means that you offer your life as an ongoing gift to the Lord. Every day we are to say, "Lord, here I am. Use me! I am a living sacrifice." "Holy" means separated unto God. I love the word "acceptable" because it means that what we offer to God has already been declared acceptable and therefore pleasing to Him. Don't you love that? God desires what you have to give Him when you make yourself available to Him.

The offering of ourselves is the beginning of all stewardship. And offering ourselves to God keeps us from being conformed to the world (12:2). It begins the process of daily transformation. When we give Him our temple (body), we are giving Him all that we are and that includes our mind. The transformation begun through the new birth is continued by the renewing of the mind. You are helping your friend continue this process of transformation as you explore together these important biblical truths. It is this continuing transformation that will enable believers to "prove" the will of God. The word "prove" means to know and do. Help your friend to celebrate their ability to accomplish the will of God for their life.

Time. All stewardship flows naturally from the offering of our bodies. But we should consciously give back to God the time He gives us. The Psalmist speaks of numbering one's days. "So teach us to number our days, that we may present to You a heart of wisdom" (90:12). Numbering our days mandates both offering our time and being accountable for how we use the time God gives us.

Paul puts the matter of the stewardship of one's time this way—"Therefore be careful how you walk, not as unwise men, making the most of your time, because the days are evil" (Ephesians 5:15-16). The stewardship of our time does not simply suggest giving time to the Lord in service through our church, although it certainly does include that. To be good stewards of time means that we view every day and every moment as a gift from God. We savor each moment as a gift from God. We seek to see God at work in all of our opportunities and join Him in His activity. The stewardship of our time makes every day a kingdom adventure.

Talk together about what it means to present our time to God. How does the stewardship of time impact our commitment to having a personal quiet time? How would it impact our commitment to give priority to service, fellowship, and worship with our church family? How can we be good stewards of time at work?

Talents. Under the matter of talents I want you to consider what you call "natural talents" and what the Scripture refers to as "spiritual gifts." You may find the topic of "spiritual gifts" a bit overwhelming, but I think we have made this topic a little more complicated than it actually is.

First, let's simply agree with the testimony of Scripture which asserts that all believers are gifted. Here's how Paul states it. "But to each one is given the manifestation of the Spirit for the common good" (1 Corinthians 12:7). We sometimes make too much of a distinction between our talents and our "gifts." God created us and redeemed us with certain good works in mind. "For we are His workmanship, created in Christ Jesus for good works, which God prepared beforehand so that we would walk in them" (Ephesians 2:10). When you give yourself to God the distinction between spiritual gift and natural talent disappears.

Spiritual gifts are "abilities" given by God which enable us to participate fully and effectively in His kingdom activity. We shouldn't get too concerned with whether those abilities were given at physical birth or after our spiritual birth; both were transformed at the moment of redemption. By the way, you shouldn't worry about whether or not your ability for service is found on any gift list. All of the gift lists were intended to be illustrative and not comprehensive. When you give yourselves to God fully, He will help you to discover the abilities that will enable you to serve Him effectively. If you aren't sure about your gifts for service, ask the Creator.

Involving your friend in gift discovery will be one of the joys of your life. You can ask simple questions to help your friend find his place in the body. When you think about the church or community, what do you see as the greatest need? What would you enjoy doing? Take your friend with you as you serve God through your gift. Urge your friend to be patient. God will show him his place in the kingdom in His own time.

Testimony. You have already seen how God can use one's testimony. You were privileged to share your own story as you led your friend to Christ. You now have the unique opportunity to help your friend understand that they have a story to tell. They may not feel capable or worthy. They may think that their story is not worth telling. It may not seem very dramatic. God gives us all a story and wants us to share it.

Remember, witness is what we *are* before it is what we *do*. In the Sermon on the Mount, Jesus declared that those who follow Him were "salt" and "light" (Matthew 5:13-14). Salt doesn't have to try to be salty, it is by nature salty. Light shines because it is its character to do so. Jesus warned that salt should not lose its flavor and light must not be hidden but set upon a hill.

Help your friend to see that they must simply let their life show whose they are and their lips explain how they came to have a personal relationship with Christ. That is the whole point behind the *SPLASH* strategy that you employed to bring your friend to Christ. Now you have the privilege of helping your friend show and tell his story to another.

You might want to study the *SPLASH* book with your friend. You should help them to learn how to tell their story. Remind them that it is an ongoing story. Encourage them to tell their story to someone else who needs to hear that story. Telling their story will not only give them personal assurance of the transformation that has taken place in their own life, it will give them the opportunity to lead someone else to a personal relationship with Christ. Offer to accompany them as they tell someone else their story.

Treasure. Don't be afraid to introduce the topic of "treasure" or "money" to your friend. The Bible speaks more often about money than it does about heaven or hell. Many people struggle with money matters and thus by sharing biblical principles, you will be helping your friend to find mastery in an area of life that plagues many people.

Immediately after the passage we call the Lord's Prayer, Jesus warned about the danger of laying up treasure on earth. He indicated that earthly treasure is fraught with frailty. Moth and rust can corrupt it, or a thief can steal it. Jesus offered a better alternative. We can invest earthly possessions in kingdom enterprises allowing us to store up treasure in heaven (Matthew 6:20-21). The miracle of Christianity is that the King allows us to use our earthly possessions (on loan from Him) to invest in heavenly treasure. What an incredible deal! We can exchange temporal and temporary "stuff" for eternal treasure.

By the way, if you continue reading in Matthew 6 you will find the word "worry" occurs five times in connection with matters such as clothes, food, and one's body. The cure for anxiety is the firm assurance that our Father already knows our needs (6:32) accompanied by our resolute focus on His kingdom and His righteousness (6:33). The stewardship of our financial resources helps us to maintain kingdom focus.

You may be wondering if the Bible tells us how much to give. The answer is "yes"—we are to give Him our all. God is concerned about how we earn money, how we spend money, how we save it and invest it, as well as how we give it. But beyond that the Bible does speak of "tithes" and "offerings." A tithe simply means a tenth or 10%. The tithe is first mentioned in Genesis 14 where Abraham joyfully gave 10% of the spoils of war in recognition that God, who possesses the heaven and the earth, had given him victory.

The tithe was later codified in Old Testament law and became normative for Israel. In the last book of the Old Testament, God accused Israel of robbing Him of the tithes and offerings that were rightfully His. Yet He challenged them to return to Him in the giving of the tithes and offerings and see if He would not open the windows and pour out a blessing (Malachi 3:10).

The tithe would have been well known to the Jewish people during the time of Jesus and thus we do not find it frequently mentioned in the New Testament. Nonetheless, when Jesus spoke of the tithe He was talking to the Pharisees, the legalists of His day. He informed them that should already have mastered elementary matters of faith such as tithing, yet without neglecting weightier matters such as justice, mercy, and faithfulness (Matthew 23:23). In other words, Jesus saw the tithe as one of the basic issues of one's relationship to God.

The tithe is a good foundation for beginning one's stewardship of treasure, but not a place to conclude. In 1 Corinthians 16, Paul spoke of proportionate giving. In other words, those who have received more have the privilege of giving more. In 2 Corinthians 8 and 9, he discussed other principles of giving such as joyous giving and grace-empowered giving which offers us both the freedom and opportunity to give beyond the tithe. By the way, "offerings," in the time of Paul, would have been understood as "gifts beyond the tithe."

You might want to study several of these texts together as a part of the discipling process. Don't think of tithes and offerings as "giving" but think of it as "investing" God's resources in His eternal kingdom. It is true that you can't take anything with you, but you can invest it in advance.

A parable of kingdom stewardship

I would suggest that you culminate your study of stewardship by looking at the parable of the talents recorded in Matthew 25:14-30. It teaches many wonderful truths—

- God willingly entrusts us with His treasure.
- God expects us to invest it well in Kingdom activity.
- There will be a time of accountability.
- There will be a wonderful day of reward.

Our reward for the stewardship of this life will be hearing our Savior welcome us with the words— "Well done, good and faithful slave" (25:21). Further, He promises that He will put us in charge of many things when we come into His presence. I don't fully comprehend these verses, but I do believe that it means how we use those things with which God has entrusted us while on earth, will determine how we serve Him for all eternity. Finally, God promises that through our stewardship we will enter into the joy of service.

Suggestions

This session suggested that you study several key texts together. Take your time as you study together and be willing to answer questions and share honestly about your own journey.

Many of the elements of this lesson will be learned through personal observation and practice. Take your friend with you as you serve through the church and share your story with other friends.

Several verses mentioned in this section would be good for memorization. Choose several to work on together.

Malachi 3:10

Matthew 6:32-33

Romans 12:1-2

1 Corinthians 3:10

1 Corinthians 12:7

Ephesians 5:15-16

If you want to study more about stewardship of money you might enjoy reading *Making Change: A Transformational Guide to Christian Money Management.* If you want to read more about spiritual gifts look for *You Are Gifted: Your Spiritual Gifts and the Kingdom of God.*

A DISCIPLER'S GUIDE

CHAPTER 6

HEART

We addressed the matter of man's heart when we talked of the Great Commandment—that we are to love God with all our heart, soul, mind, and strength. In this final section we address a related issue—the Heart of God. We look at God's passion and ask Him to create that passion in us. The bottom line—kingdom people desire most to please their King and join Him in His mission. What is that mission? To bring all nations and all peoples under His beneficent rule.

God's love for His own Creation

When we look at the opening pages of the Old Testament, we encounter the one true God creating everything that exists. It is apparent He takes pleasure in His creation, continually declaring it to be "good." I suggest that you study the opening chapters of Genesis with your friend. Don't get distracted by the details. I want you to show them the "big picture."

As you read the first chapter of Genesis draw attention to the constant repetition of the word "good"

(4, 10, 12, 18, 21, 25). When you come to the last verse of chapter one you will notice that God declares all that He made to be "very good." This means that it was pleasing to God and designed to accomplish His purpose. God created everything by design and you are part of that design.

As you read Genesis chapter one you will notice that man stands as the pinnacle of God's creation. God declares that man is made in His image and assigns to him (male and female) the responsibility of stewardship over all that He has created. To be in the image of God means that man is rational, relational, and responsible.

Man's rationality allows him to hear and respond to God's revelation of Himself. The Bible contains both the "acts" and "words" of God who chose to reveal Himself to man. Thus Bible study and prayer are essential disciplines that allow man to hear and respond to God.

God's unique revelation of Himself to man demonstrates His desire that man live in close relationship with His creator and his fellow creatures. Man's rational and relational nature makes him responsible to God. "Responsibility" requires that man seek to fully comprehend why God created him. In other words we ask, "What is our purpose during the few days of our sojourn on this planet we call earth?"

It is apparent from the creation narrative that God created man out of His infinite love and thus we exist for His pleasure and for His glory. We exist to live in intimate relationship with our Creator. Yet, we find throughout history that man has chosen to rebel against his Creator and to anoint himself king.

The rebellion of Adam and Eve clearly illustrates man's desire to be like God. Adam and Eve were allowed to live in a garden which met their every need. They were privileged to walk with God in personal intimacy. Only one tree was restricted—the tree of the knowledge of good and evil (2:17). The temptation and the desire "to be like God" (3:5) led to the first couple's rebellion and downfall. This story has been repeated by all mankind throughout history.

The Impact of Sin

We see the immediate impact of sin on man and upon the earth where he lives. Sin now shatters the first earthly family and strife and murder follow (Ch. 4). Yet throughout the story we see God's infinite love and His longsuffering character. As Creator, He could have destroyed His rebellious creation, but instead He acted redemptively. He placed man outside the garden to protect him from eating of the tree of life in this fallen state. As man continues in sin, God brings judgement followed by a promise of redemption. We can see this pattern in the account of the flood in Noah's day where judgement followed by God's promise of redemption pictured in the rainbow (Chs. 6-8).

Man proves to be a slow learner and in Genesis 11 we find him attempting to make a name for himself by building a tower to reach into the heavens (4). Man was created to make a name for God alone but his selfish desire remains focused on his own glory. This act of pride and rebellion leads to the confusion of the languages and the scattering of the nations.

God's Redemptive Plan

God calls Abram to follow Him and gives him a promise of His blessing. "And I will make you a great nation, and I will bless you, and make your name great; and so you shall be a blessing; and I will bless those who bless you, and the one who curses you I will curse. And in you all the families of the earth will be blessed" (12:2-3). Abram and his descendants are the Hebrew people. We refer to this as the Abrahamic covenant. Notice that God has chosen to accomplish His mission through human instruments.

We need to notice several components of this covenant. God promises blessing which includes His *presence*, *provision*, and *protection*. The blessing of God implies responsible mission. God desires that the blessing through Abram be spread to all the nations. God's choice of the Hebrews was not to be an *exclusive* one but an *inclusive* one. God chose and blessed Israel to enable them to join Him in reaching the nations. Tragically, the book of Genesis, which records the history of the Patriarchs (Abraham, Isaac, Jacob, and Joseph), ends with Israel in Egyptian bondage. Israel saw the call and blessing of God as *privilege* and not as *responsibility* and therefore they *consumed* God's blessing rather than *conveying* it.

A Covenant People

The event of the Exodus once again illustrates God acting to redeem His people. Israel is in Egyptian bondage. It will be helpful to read the first few chapters of Exodus with your friend. You will see that God sends Moses to be His instrument through which He delivers His people from bondage. Once again God accomplishes His mission by using human instruments.

Moses is reluctant to respond to God's invitation to be the instrument through whom He brings redemption. He views himself as unworthy and incapable. He suggests that God made a mistake in calling him and suggests that his brother would have been a better choice. No doubt you have felt both unworthy and inadequate when it comes to serving God. No doubt, your friend is having some of the same misgivings. You can point out that God promises Moses His continual presence, provision, and protection (His blessing). God doesn't ask Moses (or us, for that matter) to accomplish His work; He invites us to be the vessel through which He accomplishes His kingdom activity.

After the Israelites have been delivered from the Pharaoh's army and given safe passage through the Red Sea, Moses brings them before the Lord in the place designated by the Lord. God reminds them of His redemptive activity and then declares—"Now then, if you will indeed obey My voice and keep My covenant, then you shall be My own possession among all the peoples, for all the earth is Mine; and you shall be to Me a kingdom of priests and a holy nation" (Exodus 19:5-6).

Israel now belongs to God by *creation* and by *redemption*. As God's covenant people, they are called to obedience and holiness, enabling them to serve as a "kingdom of priests." This simply means that they are to represent the King on earth as He empowers them to reclaim the peoples of the earth. Did you notice the phrase "for all the earth is Mine"? The Bible is the story of God's plan to allow man, created in His image, to join Him in His redemption of the nations. Israel was to become a mission people. They were to embrace and manifest the heart of God for the nations.

God was seeking a people who would *embody His name, embrace His mission, and obey His word.* His heartbeat was to use this people as the instrument through whom He would bring the nations to their rightful King. Tragically, once again Israel saw the calling and blessing of God as privilege and not responsibility. They failed to manifest compassion or concern for the nations.

The Rest of the Story

I always enjoyed Paul Harvey who was best known for the line, "and now, the rest of the story." God's redemptive plan was not thwarted by man's disobedience. He sent His own Son, who is the rightful King (Messiah) of all nations to earth to redeem mankind from their sin. Jesus not only declared the message of the kingdom, He also became the means for sinful mankind to enter the kingdom.

When Nicodemus sought Jesus out because he believed him to be sent by God, Jesus said to him, "Truly, truly, I say to you, unless one is born again he cannot see the kingdom of God" (John 3:3). Man was not created to live a few years on earth and then die and cease to exist, He was created to live in fellowship with God forever. But for one to enter this kingdom, He must be born from above. We love John 3:16 which explains how one may be born again by believing in the only begotten Son of God.

What an incredible plan and message! This is the message that you had the joy of sharing with the friend you now nurture in the Lord. Now you have the joy of helping your friend understand that the message continues and that he is part of that continuing story. The kingdom of God was manifest in His Son and through our personal relationship with Him, we have now become part of the kingdom family. As a responsible family member, our task is to join God in His mission of gathering the nations.

If you look together at the disciple's prayer in Matthew 6:9-13 you will discover the restatement of God's kingdom strategy which began with Israel. Remember that God redeemed Israel so that they might embody His name, embrace His mission and obey His word? Listen—"Hallowed be Your name. Your kingdom come. Your will be done, on earth as it is in heaven" (Matthew 6:9-10). In other words, God plans to complete the process of the redemption of the earth with those who are sons of God. Kingdom citizenship is now kingdom sonship. We have become members of that community through our personal relationship with the King and as such we are called to join Him in His mission.

Membership presupposes mission

We must not repeat the mistake of Israel. We must not focus on the privilege of membership and ignore the responsibility. We must not consume God's blessings and fail to convey them.

Matthew, Mark, and Luke all end with a version of what we call the Great Commission. We know it best from Matthew's gospel. "Go therefore and make disciples of all nations, baptizing them in the name of the Father and the Son and the Holy Spirit, teaching them to observe all that I commanded you; and lo, I am with you always, even to the end of the age" (28:19-20).

The book of Acts opens with the scene of the resurrected Lord providing proof of His resurrection and teaching about His kingdom (Acts 1:3). The King then tells them that the empowering of the Holy Spirit will enable them to complete the task of taking the message to the ends of the earth. They will take the message to Jerusalem, Judea, Samaria, and to the ends of the earth (Acts 1:8). You can explain that this verse means that our mission begins in our own neighborhood but extends to the ends of the earth.

You have the privilege of showing your brother/sister in Christ that they are now part of this great mission and that they have the privilege of joining with God in the gathering of the nations. According to 1 Peter, all believers become "living stones" so they can be built up into a spiritual house for a holy priesthood to offer up spiritual sacrifices acceptable to God (2:4-12). The spiritual sacrifices that we offer to God include our bodies, our praise and worship, our giving, and our going.

I suggest that you study this passage and then *commission* your friend as a missionary. As kingdom-centered people we don't just pray for "the missionaries" we *become* missionaries. You can tell them to "quit their job" and to take it back up as a "mission assignment." Becoming a missionary means that we begin our mission where God has placed us. Our first mission assignment is to our Jerusalem. Talk about how every believer must demonstrate God's name through their behavior at work, at home, and at play. This manifestation of God's character will provide ample opportunities to "Share Him." If you have not studied *SPLASH* together, now would be an appropriate time. The *SPLASH* study will help your friend become effective at their mission assignment.

You have already begun the process of involving them in a local church. Help them to see how their mission flows through that church. Explain how your church supports others who are involved in missions around the world. If your church regularly participates in mission trips, invite your friend to accompany you on one of those trips.

Did you know that by *splashing* your friend you have made an eternal impact? Only heaven will show how many people will be impacted by the winning and discipling of one who will win and disciple others. Let's keep the process going until the King returns.

Thanks!!!

PRAYER OF JESUS

As Christians we long to be closer to God, and prayer is the avenue God has given us. In *The Prayer of Jesus: The Promise and Power of Living in the Lord's Prayer*, Dr. Ken Hemphill divides the Lord's Prayer into its component parts to show why it remains the perfect model for any believer's prayer life.

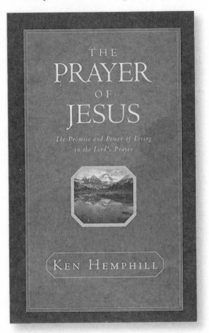

The Prayer of Jesus*
Item 978-0-8054-2567-5

**The Prayer of Jesus,
Member Book**
Item 978-0-6330-7624-4

**The Prayer of Jesus,
DVD Leader Kit**
Item 978-0-6330-7623-6

ETERNAL IMPACT

The only process that will radically transform the mission and structure of today's community of believers is the Word of God applied by the Holy Spirit. Toward that goal, *Eternal Impact: The Passion of Kingdom-Centered Communities* presents to readers a biblical study of the New Testament Church, focusing on the founding principles of the church in Matthew 16 and the birth of the church in Acts 2. Also included are chapters on the eight key characteristics of kingdom-centered churches and discussions on leadership and giftedness among church members.

Eternal Impact, Trade Book
Item 978-0-8054-4660-5

Eternal Impact, Workbook*
Item 978-1-4276-2735-3

Eternal Impact, DVD*
Item 978-1-4276-2734-6

MAKING CHANGE

Making Change presents the essential basics of money management for Christians and then casts a greater added vision to the church and individuals of how our God-given financial resources can change lives for the sake of His kingdom.

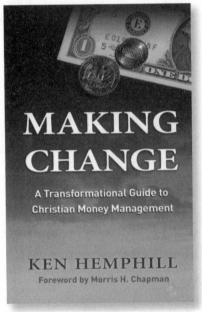

Author Ken Hemphill begins by helping readers discover the blessing of contentment rather than the gnawing curse of greed and shares helpful instructions on debt reduction, earning, saving, and spending. He also addresses the biblical laws of giving and teaches an inspiring concept of "whole-life stewardship" that can lead to a person's legacy. And that's worth more than anything money could ever buy.

Making Change, Trade Book
Item 978-0-8054-4426-1

**Making Change,
Member Book**
Item 978-1-4158-5607-9

**Making Change, DVD/CD
Multipack (Pack of 5)**
Item 978-1-4158-6012-2

Making Change, Leader Kit
Item 978-1-4158-5281-2

Making Change for Students*
Item 978-0-615-19788-3

YOU ARE GIFTED

A book about spiritual gifts is sure to address well-known gift passages and guide readers toward a greater understanding of how to find and use what God has assigned to them. Those areas are clearly discussed and then taken into an even greater context with *You Are Gifted* by respected church voice Ken Hemphill.

"The central thrust of Scripture is that spiritual gifts are graciously given by God to enable believers to participate fully in the edification of the church and the advance of the kingdom," he writes.

To that end, Hemphill reminds readers of their capability and worthiness to join in God's work.

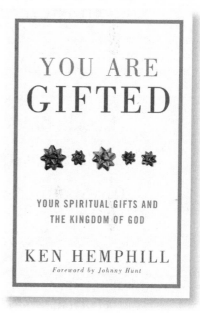

You Are Gifted, Trade Book
Item 978-0-8054-4862-4

You Are Gifted, Workbook*
Item 978-1-4276-3920-2

You Are Gifted, DVD*
Item 978-0-578-01692-4

New from Ken Hemphill…

iBelieve
in foundational truths

New book from Ken Hemphill
available for the first time at the
2010 Southern Baptist Convention
in Orlando, Florida

iBelieve in Foundational Truths is the first in the devotional gift book series BUILDING BLOCKS FOR KINGDOM FAITH. This pocket-sized book includes four-page readings that are easy to retain and share with others. These Biblical truths will help you form a firm foundation for your faith.

For more information about this
and other books from Ken Hemphill,
visit AuxanoPress.com